9-2-70

DEATH IS
ALL RIGHT

DEATH IS ALL RIGHT

GLENN H. ASQUITH

ABINGDON PRESS
NASHVILLE • NEW YORK

DEATH IS ALL RIGHT

ISBN 0-687-10327-4

Library of Congress Catalog Card Number: 79-124746

Scripture quotations unless otherwise noted are
from the Revised Standard Version of the Bible,
copyrighted 1946 and 1952 by the Division of
Christian Education, National Council of Churches,
and are used by permission.

SET UP, PRINTED, AND BOUND BY THE
PARTHENON PRESS, AT NASHVILLE,
TENNESSEE, UNITED STATES OF AMERICA

For my beloved sister
Mabel, who, with courage,
has come to terms
with death

CONTENTS

PREFACE

We don't talk much about death, do we?

We talk about the weather, about our jobs, about children and grandchildren, about the news of the day, about our plans for a vacation. As we grow older we begin to give thought to retirement, and we talk about that. But why do you and I skirt the subject of death?

For there comes a time when dodging the crowning event of life is no longer possible. We lose a family member, after we had grown accustomed to thinking that death could come into other homes but not into ours—at least not for a long, long time. Or a personal illness or narrow escape brings close the inescapable fact of our own death. The death of a friend our own age can numb us and prompt us to ask the question, "Am I next?"

As I try to come to terms with death, I am aware that the subject has been surrounded by negative attitudes in my own mind and in the minds of my associates. Perhaps we have inherited the myths and false notions of earlier generations; death and darkness have been synonymous in our thinking.

Now I have come to feel sure that I have been altogether wrong in my interpretation of death. Since I must accept eventual death for myself and for everyone whom I love and admire, and since I know that no one enters the gate of another life except by death, how can I make it a tragic happening? I have found so much beauty, so much joy, so much imagination, so much to do in life that I am beginning to comprehend that my life pattern just could not be completely altered by death.

In my pondering on death (perhaps the greatest subject that can occupy the mind of man) I have inquired, "Are there not many positive reasons to believe that death will be my helper when it comes, that death is friendly and not fearful?" A number of such reasons have occurred to me, and on the following pages I explore these conclusions. I know that I have been guided to a new outlook on death as I have meditated upon it, and I hope that everyone who reads this book will be comforted and cheered and led to thinking through the problem for himself.

GLENN H. ASQUITH

AN ADJOURNMENT

The program in my hand was rather frightening. It was the schedule of events, or agenda, for a meeting I was attending. I had left my home and familiar surroundings to come to a strange city for study and the transaction of business. But this program—how long it was! At the top of the page was the Call to Order, and then item after item stretched to the bottom of the sheet. With misgiving I turned the paper and found other listings. But there was one glorious word at the end—Adjournment! No matter how long or how short the meeting proved to be, the planner of the session had provided for a certain conclusion.

When I think of why death is all right, that meeting of years ago comes to mind. And I think of hundreds of similar gatherings. I think also of church services, concerts, plays, and classes. For each of these occasions there was a program or order of service. Between the call to worship and the benediction, between the overture and the finale, between the first curtain and the last curtain there were scheduled happenings for my participation, my enjoyment, my instruction, my enrichment. Frequently there were some that seemed to be for my endurance only! But always there was an end.

For life, too, there is a program. At the top of the first page is birth, and, following all the events intended for us, at the bottom of the last page, is death. Fortunately, we are not provided with a printed program or agenda. We do not know how long our life-meeting is to be. Some of us have short meetings and death-adjournment comes quickly; others live to experience pages and pages of life events and die as old people. Of one thing we may be sure, every life-meeting is a complete meeting. All the events intended by the Planner have been properly covered if the person involved has been faithful and patient and has not walked out on his meeting. The poets Keats and Shelley died in their twenties but left scores of beautiful and inspiring poems, whereas Grandma Moses did not come to the item of painting on her life program until she was well along in years. It is idle, then, to say of anyone, "He died before his time," or "He has outlasted his usefulness."

There is the possibility, of course, that some items on a life program may be optional depending upon what earlier years have achieved. There are times when we pick up an agenda and find that item 14-*a* will be covered *if* item 14 does not take care of the business at hand. And there are times when the reading of the minutes or the giving of reports may be dispensed with by common consent. When death comes suddenly, some item or items of life business may be dispensed with. The suffering or disability usually attendant upon the particular illness or accident that brought about death is crossed out. The meeting adjourns suddenly, but not by the omission of anything essential to completeness.

Certainly, whenever it comes, adjournment is truly a benediction (a blessing). It is much like the *coup de grâce* of old knighthood. This was the "stroke of mercy" that brought death to a desperately wounded warrior writhing in his pain. The warrior, having spent a long, hard-fought day in a battle, having received blow after hard blow, could no longer rally again to the battlecry but pleaded with his antagonist to lift the dagger and end his helpless struggle. He received his *coup de grâce*, his life's adjournment, with a sigh of relief.

Death, then, can be seen as all right when it comes as the normal conclusion to life. It should appear not as a surprise, as something fearful or dreadful, or as something unwanted, but as something that has always been plainly included on our life schedule from the day we were born. As adjournment meant for me at the close of that meeting in a strange city, so death means freedom to go home.

THE ONE COMMON EXPERIENCE

"I know just how you feel," I said to a friend who had suffered a great misfortune. But the man answered, "No, you cannot possibly know how I feel—you would have to be me to know exactly how I feel. But thanks for your sympathy." I realized that my friend had spoken truly. I could not share his experience. We try so very hard to enter into the sorrows and joys of others, and always we fail.

For instance, the ancient prophet Ezekiel saw the wretchedness of his kinsmen in captivity and thought to be at one with them. He said, "I sat where they sat and remained there seven days." But after seven days he still saw through the eyes of Ezekiel, heard through the ears of Ezekiel, and felt through the body of Ezekiel. He was still Ezekiel.

This brings us to another reason for saying

death is all right. Death is one of the inevitable experiences we have in common with the brothers and sisters around us. And this thought can be comforting. The next time I sit on a bench in an art gallery alongside another visitor and we both look at the same painting and I wonder, "Does he see in that picture what I am seeing?" I can know that we are both going forward to the same end. Death will be our common lot, even though our appreciation of other things is not the same. The leading lines of the individual's background draw taut in a forbidding way just as there would seem to be true "togetherness," but these lines relax and permit death to be the bond of humanity. Death satisfies the yearning for a bridge over the gap of loneliness and puts us into a situation that includes everyone. It is the only door of entry into our common human heritage that is stripped of all pretense and artificiality.

This truth comes home to us when we read of the passing of some greatly adored person in the world. A man or woman may have been held in such esteem throughout the world that we in our humble places have scarcely been bold enough even to dream of close companionship. But when the obituary appears in the newspapers, do we not feel suddenly closer?

The beautiful people could be listed: princes, princesses, actors, actresses, the lovely but unknown who have crossed our paths momentarily and left us breathless with their perfection of line and form and color; small children whose preciousness and freshness draw us. All of these must experience death with us.

And there are the wise of all ages: the philosophers, the astronomers, the mathematicians, the physicians, who have carried the banner of learning and insight far into the unexplored darkness and have broadened our understanding of life. These have died or will die. Some day we shall be on a level with them in our death.

We can add to them the great artists, who have painted, who have shaped stone and metal, who have designed lordly buildings, who have written books and filled museums.

How could we possibly hope to be near them except that they share death with us?

Beyond all others, perhaps, are the saintly people who have walked the paths of the world in service and in love. The ones who have spoken of faith and of courage and of God, who have drawn our desires from the temporary to the eternal—even they are not immune from death.

Is not death all right when it becomes our only way of entering into the experience of these whom we admire and who seem so far from our lowly lives?

The great mystery of death is the same for all —without gradation for the rich and the poor, the educated and the unlearned, the beautiful and the ugly, the gentle and the violent, the strong and the weak. At the moment of the end we shall know how all the others felt and they will have known how we feel. At last our sympathy, our oneness, will be complete.

RETURN TO
OUR SOURCE

"Where did I come from?" we ask as children with unerring childish curiosity. And usually we receive ridiculous and inadequate replies. Because no good answer is given to us, we go on to maturity with our question about the source of unexplained life lying on a shelf gathering dust. We look straight at the portion of life that a day brings and do not wonder where it comes from.

In our way we treat life as countless generations of Egyptians have treated the river Nile. Its abundant waters have been used for irrigation, its rich silt has made the land fertile, its broad bosom has carried boats of all kinds. But who has given a thought to the source of the Nile? It was not until John Hanning Speke came to Africa and noted that the flowing river was the very life of the country that any real concern was given to the fountainhead of the Nile. When questioned, the natives casually pointed to the far-off hills and forests and returned to their work. But Speke was not satisfied. He retraced the path of the river until, in 1862, he found where the mighty Nile was born.

As we give some thought to the source of our life, we can say death is all right since it leads us back to the fountain of our existence. Perhaps this is why some people who have come close to death, particularly by drowning, have witnessed that the events of their life came quickly to mind, beginning with the present and working back to childhood. And perhaps this is why dying men and women so often call out for their mothers instead of for their wives or husbands or children; they are on the road back to their source.

A hidden cry for the source of our being, stifled for awhile, comes to the fore at death, and gladly we begin going back up the channel of the flowing years. We long to know what it was that started us off on our earthly pilgrimage. What is it back there that is so powerful and creative that it causes life to spring forth to people around the whole earth century after century? There comes a time when we must know what this source is, and to know we must return.

This return to our source is in keeping with all nature. What we are pleased to call the lower forms of life, the trees, the insects, the animals, return in due time to their life source. We picture their destiny as far different from ours, but they serve as examples of the principle of return. Every fall season reminds us of the eternal cycle of the leaves and flowers.

Another illustration of this return to the source may be found in the young people who go abroad for study and research. A student finds his life forever enriched by his experiences and investigations. But he knows that his sojourn in strange lands is for a limited time only, and he would have it no other way. He has a native land to which he must return, and to which he will return with joy.

And will it not be vastly exciting to find out who we are and why we are by tracing our life stream to the source? This is "where the action is." Everything else is tributary and secondary. The Source is headquarters for all that life is and holds. The Power that sent us forth into the world will be discerned and known intimately. Ignorance will give way to certainty. Our life will touch The Life, and our sphere will no longer be limited by the narrow banks and twisting channels of the years we have lived.

These years have taken us farther from the beginning. The poet Wordsworth thought that we came from God "trailing clouds of glory." These clouds have been brushed off bit by bit in the skirmishes and struggles of life; the pitiless glare of the practical concerns of our days has dissipated the glory until little is left. As we return to The Source, we come closer and closer to the glory that was once ours as innocent, dreaming children, and we enter the aura where all is glory and wonder.

THE OTHER END
OF THINGS

I was ten. School was out and I had a long summer of days to do pretty much as I pleased. But from that summer only one memory has persisted and this memory recurs often. In my mind I see and feel again the browned, warm grass on a small hillock beside our house in a small town in Illinois. Ours was the last house on the street, and, as I lay on my back with my feet dangling over the bank, I could see across a field the outline of the first farmhouse. It was afternoon and the sun shone on the windows of that distant house until they appeared to be solid gold. Every element of that far-off hour of my boyhood comes back to me: the warmth of the sun on my body, the comfort of the gentle breeze riffling my hair, the odor of the grass and flowers, the merry laugh of one of my two companions, the overall drowsiness and complete lack of tension or worry. I sensed then that everything was all right, I was all right, and forever nothing would be less than all right.

Why does this one recollection come back to me repeatedly when so many other things that seemed vastly more important have long since become dulled or else vanished completely? Could it be that I had on that afternoon my message of the everlastingness and joy of life? Did there come to me a foretaste of the other end of things? My vision extended only to the farmhouse across the field, but there was ever so much beyond that house that I could not see: the rest of the state, other states, the oceans, the world! And beyond the world?

All of us have a few of these unexplainably enduring memories from some period of life that haunt us and bless us. Death is all right if we can think of it as the introduction to the other end of these bright and beautiful things. A poet has called such happenings "Intimations of Immortality." We have hints of what is to be.

In a way we are like fishermen who throw their lines into the water, hoping for some response from life they cannot see. When a welcome tug comes on the other end, the fisherman is delighted. As he reels in carefully, he is intent to see what creature will come from the water. And so we throw the line of our life into the unknown. Occasionally we get a tug such as I had on that summer day so long ago, and we know that there is something at the other end of our longing, our dreams, our aspirations. We can never be satisfied with just this end of life after we have felt a tug from the unknown. And we can never know what is at the other end until death transports us to that place.

These tugs from the other end of life come in various ways. Sometimes they come to us from persons. A popular song of some years ago had some such words as these: "And then across the crowded room you see a stranger. . . ." The song goes on to tell how the sight of that stranger changes all existence and makes the world ever so wonderful. In the face of a child or an older person something may be reflected that we know does not stop with that one who walks this earth with us. Something in a book we are reading, something in a picture in a gallery, a bit of music may open a vista to a vision and leave us changed because we have had a quick assurance of something at the other end of life.

Even negative things that throng our passage through this world may provide the experience that lifts us up to contemplation of the other part of what we are. Troubles of all kinds, the irritable dealings of anxious people with other anxious people, want, war, and frustration are so out of accord with what I felt at the age of ten in that small Illinois town that I know this is not all that is to be. Where have my happy experiences come from? Where have yours come from? What is it that is pulling at our souls? We know that it is not represented in what we see around us.

And so we see death as all right because it leads us to the other end of life: that end that will be just as wonderful as our occasional assurances have been. The little tugs will give way to one strong and loving tug, and we will gladly reel in the line of life and come to the full knowledge of what we have sensed for so long.

REPARATION

"My little nephew has had his other foot removed," a friend told me. When I inquired about the circumstances I learned that before his birth the mother of the boy had had German measles, and the baby had come into the world with deformed feet and hands. One foot was amputated and an artificial leg was substituted. Now the second foot was gone. Nothing could be done with the hands. This child's sister was normal in every way, as were the sons and daughters of the neighbors. Where is the justice in this situation?

Death can be thought of as the certain and all-right event that one day will bring this lad to an equality with the millions and millions of children born into the world with well-formed hands and feet.

Other physical lacks from birth can be listed

to make a great catalog of claims to be presented sometime somewhere by all who walk with handicaps throughout this world. It may console us who have our normal bodies to speak of "compensation." We can say that all who find themselves less well equipped than others must strive harder and, therefore, become better persons.

I know of a woman who suffers from cerebral palsy. She has struggled through college and has written a book. And we say, "How wonderful! Others with perfect health have not done so much. How happy she should be!" But then to hear her blurred speech and to see her wheeling along in a chair are proof that the compensation we admire is not enough—there must be a time of reparation. And that reparation cannot come in this life, so it is bound to be one of the gifts of death.

And there are other conditions that deserve reparation. Beyond the physical are the mental conditions. Because of brain damage at birth or for some other cause, there are those who cannot quite catch up with the verbal exchange that goes on around them. With a wistful smile and a gentle expression, the retarded wonder at what goes on around them; some try desperately to learn, and go away in despair. For these there is bound to be a bank from which they can draw the keenness and adeptness that they now lack. It is unfair that they should be bankrupt of mind forever.

Then there is the man or woman or child who has normal capacities but whose background and environment prevent his perception of the marvelous beauty and grace in the world. One such man worked hard to make his small farm produce a living for his family. His wife took summer boarders to increase their small income. One day the farmer went to pick up one of these visitors, and it was necessary to row across a small lake. While the country man toiled at the oars with his back to the west, the city man sat facing the sunset. Overwhelmed by the glory of the gorgeous colors as the sun went down, the guest cried out, "How beautiful! Oh, how magnificent!" Looking over his shoulder, the farmer saw the same lovely display of brightness on the hills, but, in astonishment he said, "Why, I don't see anything."

There was a lack within that prevented his inner being from coming into tune with a miracle. The extraordinary was ordinary. So it is with many who go to galleries and stare at pictures; with many who pick up a book that has left an earlier reader ecstatic and find nothing of excitement in it. These people seem not to know what they are missing, but that is all the more reason why they should have their moment of glad surprise when all the marvels of God and man dawn upon them in full reparation.

We know that each of us longs to be included in this reparation experience. No one of us can say that he is unhandicapped; no one is without some physical, mental, or perceptive weakness. There is no one of us who has never lagged behind in some department of life or another.

And since doctors or counselors cannot repair our defects, we are justified in expecting death to be all right as the bringer of equality.

RESTORATION

While weeping for something lost, a poetess implored the dead of all ages to assure her that when people die they get back what has gone from them and for which they have shed many tears, such as "Homer his sight, David his little lad." Death would be so welcome if blind poets could see again and grieving fathers could have their babies back again.

And why not? This is another reason why death is all right, for it must be a means of restoration. Science has attested that nothing is really lost in our universe. Energy may be changed in form, atoms may be rearranged, water may change to steam or ice or vapor, but nothing is ever gone. Why should not this principle apply to persons and their bereavements?

Our losses are well recorded in old photograph albums. "There I was," any one of us may say, "at the age of———." And we may say, "There is my best friend with me—I wonder what ever happened to him?" Further, we may remember something of how it was with us at each age, how supple and free of pain we were when we were young, how enthusiastic, how trusting, how full of dreams of great deeds to be done. And then, as the pages of the album are flipped over, one by one, we come close to the present and we may say sadly, "That picture was taken of me last September." In the meantime, between the childhood likeness and the present likeness, so much has been lost, both visibly and invisibly. Where are these youthful powers and visions and companionships? If the things that can be measured and weighed and counted are never really lost, why should these more valuable conditions and relationships be thought of as irrecoverable?

Actually, the restoration is of one's self. Homer's sight was part of him. Even in his blindness he remembered what he had seen, and he wrote of the "early, rosy-fingered dawn," and of "the wine dark sea." His sight belonged to all that he knew as beautiful. A restoration would revive his dimming memory of the morning and the dancing waves. And David's son was part of him as a father. A restoration would make his fatherhood complete and genuine. So what we look forward to is the restoring of those parts of us that have been taken away, leaving us yearning and incomplete.

An illustration may be found in the recording of voices. A thriving business has been built around the restoration of great speeches, great renditions of music, stirring words of men of the past and women of the past. Years ago these performances were recorded on old-fashioned wax cylinders. The years passed and the speakers and actors and singers died. Now the words and notes we thought had been lost forever have been transformed and renewed with great care on modern tapes and cylinders so we can enjoy and can be inspired by what was cast out on the air a generation ago. And likewise, if what we have lost has been faithfully recorded or received into a mold—death can be our hope of restoration. What can be done by earthly cleverness must speak of what can be done in the realm beyond the limitations of this present.

Happily, too, we can think of the restoration of death as extending beyond our own personal losses. We may hope to share in what has been lost by the millions who have walked with wisdom and gladness through the world. We may have said, "I wish I might have been alive in the days of Pericles," or "I wish I might have basked in the compassionate love of Jesus of Nazareth." This searching for something lost from the past is seen in our tendency to look for buried treasure. Solomon's mines, pirates' gold, a mother lode in some western mountain call man after man to prospect for that which was so rich in days gone by.

How all right death can be when thought of as the means of finding again the best that we were and had, the best that was in everyone who lived and struggled and went to find what had gone before! We shall go forth to find that what seems real now is but a faint echo of what we have sent forth.

THE PLACE
OF ANSWERS

Mystery stories are fascinating reading for young and old. There is something gripping in strange happenings and unexplained events. We know that going just before us on the pages is a character who leaves havoc or beneficence in his wake. No matter how fast we turn the pages this man or woman keeps ahead of us. And the reason we keep reading is, we know that whoever the criminal or miracle worker is, he will run out of space, and we shall catch up to him in the last chapter.

In a real sense life is a mystery story. Small mysteries are cleared up as the years go on, but the great mystery running along ahead of us cannot be solved before the last page, the last minute of life. And that last minute is death. Death, then, is all right because it is the place of answers. No author of an enthralling mystery is going to cheat the reader by stopping abruptly without an answer to the problems he has set up. Surely the Author of our life will not fail to supply the answer to our questions. Inasmuch as many things cannot be answered in this life, there must be a provision for them in death.

Our questions are many. The word "why" comes to us early in life and remains on our lips and in our minds as long as we live. The more we learn, the more we know that there is much more to learn. Truth seems always ahead of us as the days and years go on.

There are personal questions we ask ourselves. Why did I come into the world less richly endowed than many others I know? Or why did I come into the world blessed far beyond others who live in squalid parts of the world? Why did a certain misfortune have to happen to me while others went blithely through life; or why did I escape the sorrows that fell upon others? Why did my loved one have to die so young while an aged neighbor longed for death and could not find it? Why was I born? Am I accomplishing anything permanent in this world?

Other questions would be put by scientists. Is there life on other heavenly bodies? How many galaxies or universes are there beyond the reach of our instruments? Is earth dependent upon them in one way or another? Where did we miss the secret of the cure for cancer? What is it in man that defies X rays, blood tests, and other analyses and expresses itself in indomitable striving for higher things?

Theologians ask themselves, "Which of my doctrines and teachings are nearest divine truth?" Or, "Have I missed the road completely?"

Less important questions plague others. A scholar who specializes in Shakespearean lore has reconciled himself to waiting until the hereafter to know who really wrote the famous plays!

We may be sure that death is the only place to find the answers to the major and minor questions that have come into our life: the questions that can never yield to the probing and curious research of man. This thought of death as the place of answers seems to be the natural assumption of many. How frequently we hear mourners say of one who has just died, "But he knows now how much I loved him!" Or, "I guess I need not feel so guilty—she knows now why I could not come to her sooner." Through history many have resorted to the use of mediums and spiritualists to bring up the spirits of the dead. Why? Because it has been assumed that the dead *know* all the answers.

In any event, as we get more and more involved in the mystery of life, we can more patiently enjoy the good things and endure the hard things knowing that each happening has a meaning which will be revealed. We can train ourselves to be more alert to pick up the clues scattered through the days: the clues that will help us to have some faint idea of what may be coming. Only it will not do to turn impulsively to the last pages of the story—that would spoil the grand intent of the Author.

THE REDEMPTION
OF PROMISES

The teacher gave me a seed, and she placed a seed on the desk of each boy and girl in the second grade. And she promised that if we would plant the seed in a pot filled with soil from the schoolyard, and if we would see that the pot was placed in a sunny spot, and if we would sprinkle the soil with just enough water from day to day, a flower would grow for us! I can still remember the thrill that came to me when the soil began to crack and a tiny bit of green was seen; the teacher's promise was about to be redeemed.

I have found many promises of this kind in my life and in the life of the world at large. In the realm of nature every sunrise promises a sunset, and every sunset a sunrise. At every high noon there is the promise of dusk and dark. At every midnight there is the promise of dawn and daylight. Summer promises fall, fall promises winter, winter promises spring. Every mountain promises a valley, and every valley a hill.

Chemists, physicists, mathematicians live their lives by promises that have been given through the ages. For instance, water always comes when hydrogen and oxygen are combined in the proportion of H_2O. A man can step on the moon if certain rules are followed. If a ball is tossed on the floor at an angle, it will bounce off in the opposite direction at the same angle.

The natural and material world is full of promises that are regularly and faithfully redeemed. But what of the promises in my life and yours? Have all these been redeemed? And if they have not, will they ever be made good? Here is where death is all right as the redemption of promises.

These are the seeds we sow in life. The wisdom of the ages, the hard findings of mankind through trial and error, the teachings of great thinkers, the revelation that we think is sent from a divine source assure us that the seeds we sow and tend will surely grow. Love is a seed that has the promise of peace; hard work is a seed with the promise of success; faith is a seed with the promise of sight. But though we sow these seeds diligently, we may go through life without the thrill of seeing the breaking of the hard soil of the circumstances that contain us. Peace, true success, the attainment of the good for which we have hoped elude us. Where is the redemption of the promises? We know that the promises are too well documented to be false—in our hearts we know them to be true. And if we cannot have redemption in this life, redemption can only come at death.

The midnight of our souls must give way to a dawn somewhere. Our combining of the elements of high endeavor must eventually add up to the water of life. Our following of the rules of unselfishness and integrity must bring us to our star in time. What we cast out into the world of the best we have cannot fall inert but must bound away with the same angle of the motive with which we started it.

Without a redemption time and place, life would be dreary indeed. It would be much like the prospect of the homesteaders on western lands. The government promised them that if they would make the long, toilsome journey to the virgin forests and fields miles from their old homes, they would be given land capable of producing food in great abundance. But suppose that these would-be homesteaders had crossed the mountains and swollen streams only to find that there was no such land as their government agents had promised? Suppose that they had found the whole thing to be a tragic fraud?

Unless the promises that echo in our hearts and souls have a sure chance of redemption, we are being defrauded. But there must be this sure chance. We are not dealing with a small seed in a small pot that we can watch day after day; we are dealing with great immensities. We are sowing and combining on an eternal scale. The arrows of hope that we shoot from our bow of faith go out beyond the horizon. The few years we have to spend on earth are not enough for us to gather in the results of all that we do and believe. Death leads us to the marks that our shafts have struck.

THE OPENED STOREHOUSE

So often we stand before the display windows of a great multistoried department store. We look at the tastefully arranged and enticing samples of merchandise in the display cases, and wonder at all that must be available inside. In our mind's eye we see the thousands and thousands of beautiful and useful items that must be arranged on floor after floor. But we have arrived before opening time, and we must content ourselves with viewing the few representative articles behind the glass.

In life we have this same experience. The world is a small planet compared with the immensities of space and the size of other heavenly bodies that astronomers have measured. And yet our world shows us exquisite samples of a Creator's skill and wealth. But while this life lasts we are too early for the opening of the doors of the great storehouse.

And in our inner being we receive tokens of love, intimations of greatness, rainbows of unutterable peace that are samples of something we cannot find as we walk and search day after day. We know that we have been given glimpses in the display windows of some great and unlimited treasure. But we seem to be too early for the opening of the storehouse doors.

To use another illustration, there are times when we are allowed to take a small taste of something that has been prepared for a later meal: a tiny bit of cake, a half-teaspoonful of frosting, some crumbs from crusty bread, a sliver of turkey. These bites arouse our appetites. If they are this delicious, what must the whole menu be like! But it is too early yet to find out.

And so we say that death is all right, because it is the time of the opening of the storehouse. We know that this time must come. What merchant would content himself with nothing but display windows and have nothing inside for the eager customers to explore and take? For all of us who inhabit this little globe, there must be the knowledge that what we see and hear and feel must be extremely limited. We cannot believe that we are being tantalized with no hope of a time when we can roam at will in the main store of creation.

And we know that there must be a time when the little swatch of truth that has come to us can be matched to the great bolt from which it came; that the tiny experience of pure love will lead to a sparkling fountain of fellowship and understanding; that the unalloyed peace that visits us on rare occasions will be seen to fit into a little crevice of a great crystal of eternal accord; that all the samples of good that come to us will be verified by an endless stock somewhere.

Also, the time must come when the meal that we have been waiting for will be served. We have had our small bites of sweetness and joy and achievement and hope and companionship and all that we class as "making life worthwhile." But the tastes leave us even hungrier than before, and we know full well that these sampling bites came from the larger piece.

Thus, we can see no other time or place for our going beyond the display windows into the storehouse than death itself. We cannot believe that we shall be left as children around a Christmas tree without packages or at a holiday table with empty plates. We have our display windows for a purpose, we are given samples for a purpose, we are handed bites for a purpose. And that purpose is that we may be prepared for unspeakable riches beyond and come to the end of our quest with a sense of familiarity, even in the presence of awe. That purpose is to prove to us that this part of our life is, of itself, nothing but a foretaste of the life that is to be.

A FOCUS

"Mother, there's a cat on the fence way over there. And do you see the car parked way down the street? It has a red license plate—and I can read that street sign. 'Allen Avenue.' Oh, I never knew there were so many things to see!"

My son had just been fitted with glasses to correct his nearsightedness. His mother was bringing him home on the bus, and he was able to focus on distant objects for the first time in his life. Until he was in the second grade in school no one had discovered his visual handicap. From the day he began to wear his spectacles life became magnified and beautiful.

But there is a defect of seeing that affects all of us and that can never be corrected by earthly means. Life can be just so large and just so beautiful when it is seen only partially.

And it cannot be seen in its entirety until death provides the complete sight.

There is the great scope of life, for instance. We look at it as a photographer looks at a tremendous sweep of territory that covers far too much area for the small camera in his hands. He does his best by attaching a "wide angle" lens and by moving the camera in a panoramic fashion; sometimes he takes part of the picture in one direction and part in another, and then pastes the parts together. Even so, all that was before him is not included in the resulting print. And it is so with us. Life is too big in all its meaning to be seen fully and completely with the eyes of our present understanding.

Even when life is broken down in pieces, we find it not by any means capturable. Misfortunes come to us, and we cannot see where they fit into the great scheme of things. We miss the pieces on either side of the catastrophe that has come to us. Thus we miss the meaning. The edges of our small or great disaster blur into something that eases the pain, but we cannot see far enough to determine the why of failures and losses and sorrows. Joys, too, have the same quality of suggesting that they are parts of something greater and not just special happenings without reference to yesterday or tomorrow.

And this reminds us of the years that come to us and go. We have inner vision to see today and to catch a brief, corner-of-the-eye glimpse of the day that has just passed but we cannot gather in tomorrow. Time is just so vast that our sight is not prepared to see it as a whole. People we have known have drifted out of our line of vision. Where have they gone? Once we could gather them in along with others who walk and talk with us now.

And so we turn to death—death which is all right—to enlarge our vision so that we can see all things past, present, and future and can realize the immensity and glory of the life that has been, and is, ours. Instead of needing to adjust the binoculars of our inner sight in order to bring into focus near things or far things, we shall find that all things are constantly and clearly in focus. By concentrating on the far we do not lose a sharp view of the near. And we shall verify what we have a suspicion of now, that if all events and purposes and plans and events could be seen as one great whole there would be nothing to fear, nothing to draw away from. When death comes with the gift of true focus, reason and purpose will be the frame around all that is before us, behind us, and around us.

If it were not so, if death did not bring everything into sharp focus, there would be no point in having eyes at all; there would be no reason for loveliness and order to exist endlessly without any to see and admire somewhere.

Thought of in a material way, sight was made clearer by the two men who were first to step on the moon. The pictures and rock samples they brought back extended the vision of the telescope. And yet there is so much beyond the moon! Every truth that opens up before the eyes of the mind simply points to more in the distant shadows. Only death can make us see the fullness of what the term "life" holds.

THE REASON FOR
LIFE PREPARATION

In earlier days a boy or girl would be "apprenticed" to a master in some craft or trade. For seven years or more the learner would watch the master and would attempt to acquire the methods and the skill that he saw used so well. Then, after the long, drudgery-filled time was faithfully rounded out, the apprentice—now a young man or young woman— went forth, free to ply his trade.

Everyone of us has had, or is having, his apprentice period. No one is born with a magical endowment that permits him to avoid the trial-and-error method of working at something until he is a master of something worthwhile.

Indeed, for many pupils, almost one fourth of life is spent in schools that prepare them to go out into the world with some ability to offer in exchange for food, shelter, and clothing. Even the most advanced machines and electronic devices cannot free us of this need for learning. Perhaps we may say that the more advanced our material civilization becomes, the longer our children are required to spend in classrooms in order to cope with their more complicated world.

Even more important than our preparation to use our hands and brains to advantage is the lifelong gathering of compassion, forbearance, and understanding that makes it possible for us to live with others in joy and harmony.

But what is the purpose of all this costly and tedious preparation? How shall we put to use all that comes to us day by day? And what of the enlightenment and vision that comes to us unbidden as a result of suffering or loss? Without death there would be no answer to this question. Death is seen as all right when it is recognized as the reason for life preparation.

Otherwise how can we see any sense to a man's or woman's becoming more and more competent to do a chosen task and to live more and more graciously in a family and community, only to be cut down by disease, accident, or age? Must we think that all the person had garnered is complete waste, since he cannot use it anymore or pass it on to others? Nothing else in life points to this kind of mockery, so why should we think this is an exception?

In a sense, we might consider that what we do in this short life is the building of the model of what we are prepared to do later on a large scale. Just as an architect uses small bits of material to put together a model of a house or church or public building, so we use the small bits of our learning and understanding to bring forth a small-scale model of what our life and achievement is to be somewhere. Only a doll could occupy a little model of a home; it is not big enough for a man or woman. And the best that we can do with our time and skills here is surely far too small for the real self within to occupy forever. The potentials of our lives must be realized in fullness or we are wasting much effort in our eager design.

Another illustration of this exploration for

purpose is found in the want ads in the employment section of a newspaper. Men and women of many abilities list their training and their experience and ask for a place to use what they know. Sooner or later, each of these people will find a position or opportunity. But suppose that one well-qualified person never finds a place to work at his profession or trade? Would we not think that that man had wasted years and dollars just to be rejected by the world?

In a way, each of us fills in a want ad day by day as our experience gives us more and more reason to expect that life will permit us to use all that has come to us over the years. It is impossible to think that there will be no answer to our want ad, that we must accept the fact of being brushed aside as unneeded.

Since death comes to the young who have just completed their training before they have time to use their knowledge, and to the aged just as they are at the peak of their master's skill, we must hope that death is the opening of a door: the last and perfect answer to the soul's want ad, the reason for all our striving.

A GLAD ENCOUNTER
WITH GOD

When a man wishes to disappear in the
world, he is careful to leave no traces behind
him. He removes his name from articles of
clothing and other personal possessions. He
uses an assumed name. He disguises his appear-
ance. If he feels that he might be followed in
open country he takes a leafy bough and covers
up the tracks he has made, or he walks in water.
His aim is to make it impossible for anyone to
know of his passage from place to place.

But when a man wants to be found by his
friends who are on the road behind him, he
takes great pains to leave signs. He may drop
bits of paper to leave a trail. Or he may cut
blaze marks on trees or bend down branches.
He may leave small piles of stones here and
there. Where he can, he deliberately makes im-

pressions of his feet as he walks or runs along.

God is like the man who wants to be found. From the beginning of man's history God has wanted to be discovered by every succeeding generation. And God has left undeniable proof of his having been in the world before us.

Some of the clues we find are the wonders of the earth, the sky, and the water. No matter where the eye turns there is indescribable beauty and mystery. Things and powers that are beyond man, even with his great scientific abilities, are as common as sand on the seashore. Glaciers, deep canyons, crevasses, lake beds and riverbeds are all gigantic footprints.

Other indications of God are found within us as strange and noble thoughts and longings come to us unbidden. The illogical urge that comes over us to give of ourselves, at whatever cost, to great causes and rescues of humanity speaks of something that has not come to us through the bread and meat we have eaten.

And so we see the signs of the one we have come to call God. Exuberantly at times, wearily at times, hopelessly at times, we go our way after God. But only when death comes do we really catch up to him.

Thus death is all right because it is a glad encounter with the one whom we have doubted, to whom we have cried out in danger or despair, whom we have sought secretly or openly all the days of our lives. Suddenly we shall be face to face with God. No other life experience can be equal to this experience. Of course, this encounter must be far beyond human imagining, but, perhaps, we may use some of our terms to get a faint glimmer of what is in store for us.

We could think of death as coming in from an icy night to a warm, lighted room where someone has prepared every cheer and comfort.

We could think of ourselves as clocks that have run more and more slowly year by year and with less and less accuracy, clocks that will now be wound tight forever and set exactly right forever.

We could think of hate and apprehension as flowing out of us in the presence of pure love.

61

We could think of ourselves as having made a lifelong journey with countless changes of trains and planes, with long delays and back-trackings made to hear at last the announcement of our home station and journey's end.

We could think of ourselves, dragging along with some infirmity that doctor after doctor has tried in vain to cure, now being ushered into the treatment room of the one physician who is able to set us upright in wholeness.

In any event, we can know that the final unraveling of the mystery of God can be only good. The hints and the symbols and unfinished handiwork that we have followed all our lives have all pointed to one who is magnificently good and of matchless integrity.

So by death we come at last to the God of whom we have heard, and read, and dared to dream. We shall be amazed, of course, but we shall not be disappointed. The cry of our hearts —which our minds have tried in vain to stifle— for a God great enough to have made us people of an unsatisfied longing will find its answer in peace.

CONCLUSIONS

We have looked at the reasons why our hearts tell us that death is all right. But to be completely all right, death must be fairly earned.

Death, earned? Yes, because death is God's final benefit. How, then, does a person earn death? By accepting his place as a contributing factor in the life of the world, a person can earn death. Death will come to him in the wear and tear of the years, by accident, or by some disease that he braves in common with his fellows.

Or a person may find his place in the forefront of some essential struggle for the uplift and enlightenment of mankind. Here he will earn death earlier and, possibly, by some violent force.

Or one may take all the chances that a normal

response to life brings and earn death only by going all the way down the road of age.

Death, to be all right, must not be hurried or grasped prematurely. A person must not use death as an escape from life's obligations. In the plan of the Eternal, death in these ways may come around all right, but we have been given little insight into this complexity. We can only trust that it may be so.

As we continue then to pass the dayposts and yearposts that mark off our lives, we shall not grieve unduly when the road of a loved one no longer runs alongside ours, since, for him or her, death is all right. And as we come to the brow of that last hill of ours and death is there to embrace us, we shall not be afraid.